A journey through

GLOUCESTERSHIRE
& THE COTSWOLDS

JARROLD

GLOUCESTERSHIRE AND THE COTSWOLDS

Gloucestershire, in England's heartland, can surely be described as one of her most beautiful counties. Much of it has a gentle, rural feel, and there is enough variety of landscape and architecture to satisfy the most demanding explorer. There are stone cottages in Cotswold villages, and half-timbered buildings and magnificent churches in the 'wool towns'. Wooded hills overlook the Severn and the Wye and cover the broader expanses of the lower Severn Valley and the Vale of Gloucester. There are extensive limestone grasslands above spectacular gorges where hills plunge down dramatically on the great western escarpment of the Cotswolds; and small comfortable towns like Stow-on-the-Wold, Tetbury and Moreton-in-Marsh contrast happily with the ancient city of Gloucester and its neighbours Cheltenham and Cirencester. And then there are the gardens – Hidcote Manor, Westbury Court

and Barnsley House possess some of the country's most pleasing gardens, and the splendid arboreta at Batsford and Westonbirt should not be missed.

The Romans were the first to find the Gloucestershire area important and to leave a legacy still in use today. The Fosse Way crosses the county from east of Tetbury, through Cirencester, to north of Moreton-in-Marsh; Ermin Street and Icknield Street run through it and Akeman Street joins the Fosse Way just north of Cirencester. There are other legacies of the Romans at Chedworth Roman Villa, which dates back to about AD 120, and at the Corinium Museum, Cirencester. Daniel Defoe, in 1727, had an interesting explanation of how Akeman Street got its name: 'by the Saxon way of joining their monosyllables into significant words, as thus, *ackman*, a man of aching limbs . . . So Ackmanstreet was the road or street

for diseased people going to Bath [to seek a cure].'

The sons and daughters of Gloucestershire are as diverse as its attractions. Edward Jenner, one of the founders of modern immunology, was born there in 1743 and discovered the smallpox vaccine. His home, now a museum, is next to Berkeley Castle. Sir Peter Scott, artist and ornithologist, set up the Wildfowl and Wetlands Trust at Slimbridge. Laurie Lee, the writer famous for *Cider with Rosie*, lived at Slad and wrote nostalgically of his boyhood in the Cotswolds. Dorothea Beale, the Victorian pioneer of women's education, founded the world-famous Cheltenham Ladies' College, and W. G. Grace, the cricketer, played for Gloucestershire and England, scoring 1,000 runs in a month in 1885.

From Saxon times wool was at the heart of Gloucestershire's prosperity. Its economic success was assured by the port of Gloucester being so conveniently placed for export and trade. The docks are no longer used for their original purpose but have been converted into a wonderful storehouse of museums in which a bygone age is recaptured. Evidence of the wool trade still exists in the Cotswold towns and villages where the wool merchants lived and left a delightful heritage of buildings in warm, Cotswold stone. And sheep still graze peacefully on the Cotswold Downs.

Each of Gloucestershire's three regions – the Cotswolds, the Severn Valley and the Royal Forest of Dean – has corners well worth exploring. The pages of this book can show only a few.

1 Chipping Campden, one of the great Cotswold wool towns of the Middle Ages

THE COTSWOLDS

The Cotswolds are not conveniently contained by county boundaries. They are partly in Oxfordshire, Warwickshire and Hereford and Worcester, but largely and most characteristically in Gloucestershire. The combination of idyllic stone villages and small towns set amidst a gentle, rolling countryside is quintessentially 'English' – a result of stone, sheep and a lack of coal deposits.

The builders of the large number of long barrows here, such as Hetty Pegler's Tump in the south and Belas Knap above Winchcombe in the north, may have been sheep-herders, to judge from the bones found in the tombs.

The Romans built important roads that passed along the Cotswolds, and Cirencester was Roman Britain's second city. Chedworth Villa is a fine example of a Roman country retreat which reveals a complete community, the chief industries of which were dyeing and fulling.

The monastic foundations of the Cotswolds at Cirencester and Hailes (near Winchcombe) helped to pioneer the development of the wool trade in an age when the church was wealthy and needed to be successful to sustain its wealth. Few of the great abbeys are left because of Henry VIII's dissolution of the monasteries in 1539, but by that time the manufacturing of woollen cloth had expanded so much that it was England's major export industry, half of it being produced in the Cotswolds.

In Cirencester, Tetbury, Fairford, Northleach, Stow-on-the-Wold and Chipping Campden there are splendid houses that belonged to wool merchants and magnificent 'wool churches' built by them. In all the picturesque Cotswold towns and villages the different ages of architecture blend harmoniously. Medieval, Tudor and Georgian buildings stand side by side and are unified by the use of Cotswold stone.

The lack of coal deposits in the area did not allow the Cotswolds to develop during the Industrial Revolution as many other parts of the country did and the area lost out to the more powerful woollen industries of Yorkshire. The hardship and poverty that was suffered by the inhabitants of the Cotswolds meant that there was no money for development, so everything remained as it had been. Later, the permanent advantages of climate, countryside and accessibility made the Cotswolds an attractive place to live in and to visit. It has now been designated an Area of Outstanding Natural Beauty.

The Gloucestershire Cotswolds contain the most spectacular views of the area all along the western scarp from Hetty Pegler's Tump between Uley and Nympsfield, up past Stroud and Painswick to Birdlip and beyond. Behind the escarpment is the typical rolling wold country (*wold* is a Saxon word meaning upland and 'cot' may have come from Cod, a Saxon chief in the upper Windrush valley). In the north the Evenlode, Windrush, Leach and Coln rivers have cut lovely, wide valleys where they flow to meet the Thames.

The great castles of Berkeley and Sudeley, the Regency charm of Cheltenham and the historic city of Gloucester are all within easy reach of the Cotswolds.

2 Springtime daffodils by the church at Eastleach Turville

3 Part of the fascinating collection of town and country items from bygone days in the Woolstaplers Hall, Chipping Campden. In the fourteenth century the hall was built by a woolstapler (merchant) who probably came from London to buy Cotswold fleeces

4 Chipping Campden is an attractive market town ('chipping' means market) whose prosperity was built on wool. Some of the wealthiest wool merchants in England lived here and the houses and cottages reflect this, especially Grevel House in the main street

5 Thatch and Cotswold stone tiles were used to roof cottages in Chipping Campden. Oriel, dormer and mullioned windows, with medieval monastic-looking doorways, give a good impression of how richer market towns would have looked in the Middle Ages

6 Hidcote Manor Garden is one of the most delightful gardens in England and consists of a series of small gardens within the whole

7 Moreton-in-Marsh is a busy market town. The bell in the old Curfew Tower was once used to summon the fire brigade

8 Lord Redesdale laid out Batsford Arboretum in the 1880s on the slope of a Cotswold spur. It contains more than 1,200 species

10 Wrong-doers in bygone days were put in these stocks at Stow-on-the-Wold

Market Square in Stow-on-the-Wold, once he most thriving wool market in England. wo annual fairs, dating from 1476, are still eld here, mainly for horses

11 The Cotswold Farm Park has the most comprehensive collection of rare breeds of British farm animals in the country, displayed in a farm setting, high on top of the Cotswold Hills, near Guiting Power

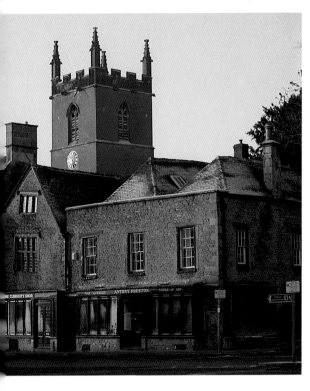

12 The narrow curving streets of Stow-on-the-Wold abound in antique shops and art galleries. This one leads down from the church and is flanked by many fine stone houses and cottages

13 A corner of Stow-on-the-Wold where the characteristic façade of stone houses is most attractive. Stow saw a particularly vicious Civil War battle in 1645, when the Royalists were so badly defeated that the street ran with blood

14 These cottages are typical of the mellow picture-postcard charm of Upper Slaughter. The grim-sounding name comes from the Anglo-Saxon word *slohtre* which has nothing to do with death and destruction, but means 'muddy place'

15 St Peter's Church, Upper Slaughter, dates from Norman times but was substantially restored in 1877. Francis Edward Witts, the rector from 1808 until 1854, has a canopied tomb here. His *Diary of a Cotswold Parson* was published in 1978

16 Lower Slaughter is the 'twin' of Upper Slaughter. Both villages are as beautiful as any in the Cotswolds with their rich, honey-coloured stone buildings that blend into the rolling Gloucestershire countryside. The River Eye runs through them

17 The early nineteenth-century corn mill in Lower Slaughter worked until the 1960s and retains its water-wheel. It now houses the Mill Museum and Shop, containing memorabilia of village life and handmade goods for sale

18 Many of the buildings in Lower Slaughter date from the sixteenth and seventeenth centuries, and some are relatively new, having windows with stone mullions and small rectangular panes edged with lead

19 The 'water' at Bourton-on-the-Water is the River Windrush which flows gently through the village under low stone bridges. The riverside path leads to quiet corners and secluded lanes

20 In 1937 the landlord of the Old New Inn built a replica to one-ninth scale of the village of Bourton-on-the-Water. Even the trees are to scale; there is a model of the model village itself, and music comes from the churches

21 First impressions are often deceptive, especially at Folly Farm which seems to be just a quaint working farm. In fact, it is Europe's largest waterfowl and wildfowl conservation area, covering some 50 acres and housing 160 different breeds, including Indian Runner ducks, pictured here

22 A modern-day harvest scene high in the Cotswolds near Northleach, which was once one of the prosperous wool towns of the Cotswolds and offers a variety of historic attractions

23 Timber-framed houses, sixteenth-century almshouses, a seventeenth-century manor house and a magnificent fifteenth-century 'wool' church containing some of the country's finest brasses, are among the treasures of Northleach

24 Harding's World of Mechanical Music in the High Street, Northleach, is a museum with a difference in a seventeenth-century merchant's home. It contains a collection of antique clocks, music boxes and mechanical musical instruments

25 The Cotswold Countryside Collection is a museum of Gloucestershire rural life housed in an eighteenth-century country prison, the design of which was copied by Pentonville prison

26 Tradition is continued in the fields of Northleach, where
sheep still graze, enclosed by Cotswold stone walls

27 Chedworth Roman Villa, near Yanworth, is one of
the best preserved Romano-British sites in England

28 This row of cottages in Arlington Row, Bibury, was
a weaving factory in the seventeenth century

29 The River Coln runs through Bibury which was once a famous horseracing centre and home of England's oldest racing club. William Morris thought it was the most beautiful village in England

30 The magnificent Parish Church of St John the Baptist stands on Market Place, Cirencester. The church has a fine collection of communion plates, including the famous Ann Boleyn cup

31 Cirencester Park, a 3,000-acre estate owned by Lord Bathurst, is open to the public for riding and walking. The eighteenth-century poet, Alexander Pope, helped to lay it out

32 Market Place has been on the same site for 300 years, but the covered market for corn and cheese on Corn Hill was built in the nineteenth century. The cattle market is in Tetbury Road

33, 34 An old brewery in Cricklade Street is now the home of Cirencester Workshops, where it is possible to watch a variety of crafts being practised. Craftsmen and women run independent businesses to produce goods on commission and for general sale

35 The Corinium Museum, Park Street, Cirencester, contains one of the country's most extensive collections of Roman artefacts. This reconstruction of a Romano-British trichinium, or dining room, is based upon the 'Four Seasons' mosaic floor

36 The Head of Neptune, from the 'Hunting Dogs' mosaic floor ound in 1849, is one of the Roman treasures on display in the Corinium Museum

37 (overleaf) The home of Lord Bathurst, which is not open to the public, is hidden by a spectacular 12-metre (40 ft)-high yew hedge planted in 1818

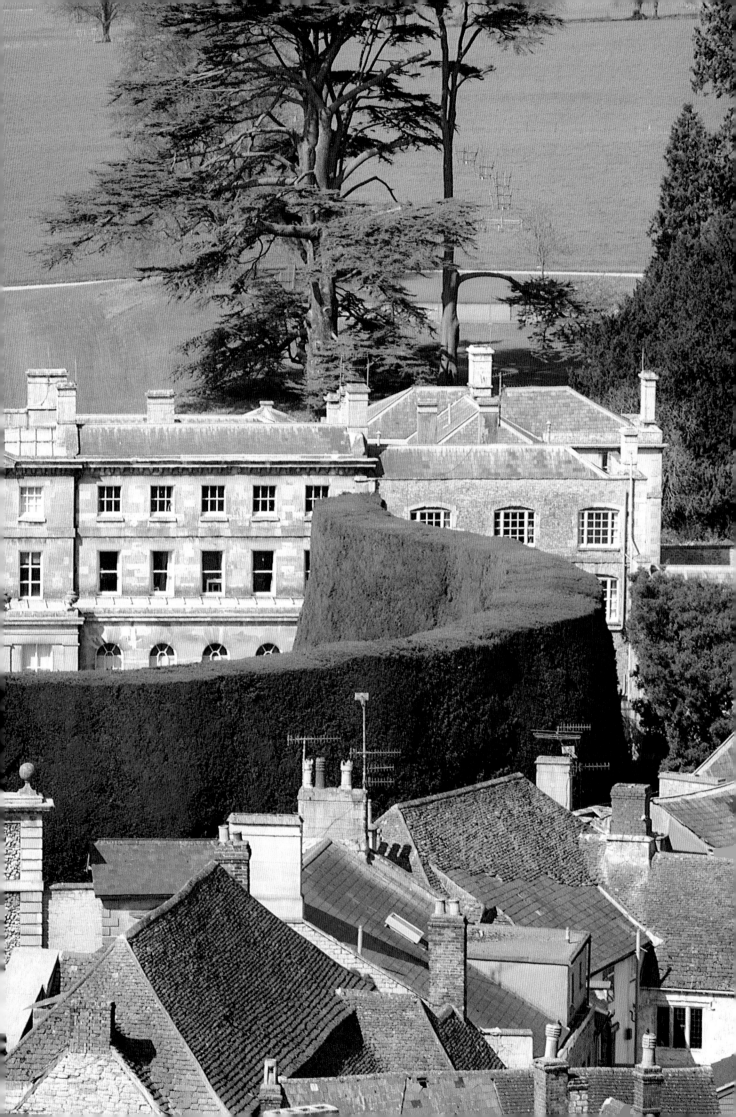

38 (far left) Painswick, 'Queen of the Cotswolds', is packed tightly with stone cottages, often lining steep, cobbled streets

39 (centre) The Table Tombs in St Mary's churchyard, Painswick, are described in *Tomb Trail*, available in the County Library

40 (left) The Market House at Tetbury, one of the southern Cotswold wool towns

41 (below) The arboretum at Westonbirt House, with its fine collection of temperate trees and shrubs, is open daily, all year round

42 The Sheldon Tapestry is one of the finest treasures in the collection of Sudeley Castle. It was made in the late sixteenth century in Warwickshire during a time of great prosperity in England

43 Off the A417 between Cirencester and Cheltenham is the scenic route to Birdlip with its breathtaking view down towards the Severn Vale

44 Sudeley Castle mirrors in its walls a thousand years of English history. It has seen good and bad times, including 200 years of neglect and ruin, but in the nineteenth century it was restored to beauty and its treasures put on display

45 Just outside the village of Uley is Owlpen Manor which used to be famous for its yews. North of Uley is the famous Stone Age barrow known as Hetty Pegler's Tump, one of the best-preserved Cotswold barrows

46 Belas Knap is another Neolithic burial mound, situated in high country south of Winchcombe

THE SEVERN VALLEY

The Severn is a river of 'infinite delights'. It winds peacefully through Tewkesbury, the northern gateway to the Cotswolds, through the once-busy port of Gloucester and, widening as it goes, merges into the Bristol Channel. On its way it passes through lush green pastures whose rich red soil supports cattle and wheat. This peaceful river can be cruel, however, when the tidal bore, a solid wall of water up to a metre (3 feet) high, rushes up its course from the sea. Adventurous surfers are keen to take advantage of the Severn bore, but it has its dangers which they ignore at their peril.

At the southern end of the vale is the late Sir Peter Scott's world-famous Wildfowl and Wetlands Trust at Slimbridge. An internationally recognised breeding station for wildfowl, it is open all year round and there is always plenty to see. 'Swan Lake' may have as many as 2,000 birds on it in winter. Almost all are wild migrants attracted by the tame birds and the food.

To the south of Slimbridge is the well-preserved medieval castle of Berkeley, where Edward II was so brutally murdered; his tomb is in Gloucester Cathedral.

North-east of Slimbridge is Prinknash Abbey where wildlife of a different variety can be seen in the Bird Park. There, fallow deer and pygmy goats wander freely among peacocks and crown cranes, and the Golden Wood is home to pheasants and the Haunted Monk's Fish Pond which is stocked with trout.

On the opposite bank of the Severn, in a quite different mood, lies Westbury Court Garden, which possesses a very rare example of a formal Dutch-style garden, the earliest of its kind surviving in England.

The ancient cathedral city of Gloucester, the Regency spa town of Cheltenham and the medieval wool town of Tewkesbury provide the urban attractions of the Severn Valley.

47 Cooper's Hill is a fine vantage point on the Cotswold escarpment for views westward across the Severn Vale

48 The River Severn at Tewkesbury with the Abbey tower in the background. The Avon meets the Severn in this northern gateway to the Cotswolds, which saw one of the worst battles of the Wars of the Roses on 'the Bloody Meadow', south of the town

49 Tewkesbury Abbey is one of the country's largest parish churches. After the Dissolution the townspeople bought it from Henry VIII for £453 and saved it from destruction

50 The massive Norman pillars in Tewkesbury Abbey support the early fourteenth-century vaulting. Daily guided tours are given to describe the fourteenth-century stained glass and many medieval monuments

51 Since it became a fashionable Regency spa town, people
have come to Cheltenham to relax and enjoy themselves

52 Neptune's Fountain, on the Promenade, where some of
the best examples of intricate iron 'lacework' in
Cheltenham can be seen

53 In the heart of Cheltenham is Montpellier, a historic Regency area with restaurants, cafés, bars and many specialist shops

54 Pittville Pump Room is Cheltenham's finest Regency building, where visitors can 'take the waters'

55 The Devil's Chimney, on Leckhampton Hill, is a remarkable 150-year-old man-made limestone outcrop. It stands high above the main road at Birdlip, restored by Cheltenham Borough Council who hope that it will stand for another 150 years

56 Joseph Pitt, a self-made man, became rich enough as a solicitor to build the Pittville Pump Room within beautiful gardens, seen here from the air

57 Gustav Holst was born in a Regency house in Cheltenham which is now a museum. It contains Holst's concert piano and personal memorabilia, and has several rooms furnished in Regency and Victorian style

58 The fine Perpendicular tower of Gloucester Cathedral rises above the old city and dominates it. Among its treasures is the tomb of Edward II

59 The magnificent fan vaulting in the great cloister of Gloucester Cathedral

60 The east window in the Cathedral commemorates the valiant deeds of local knights and barons at the Battle of Crécy (1346) and is a splendid backdrop to the high altar

61 At Gloucester Docks the disused warehouses of yesteryear have been transformed to meet today's appetite for boats, museums, restaurants, pubs, antiques and specialist shops

62 The Chemist's Shop in the Robert Opie Collection at Gloucester Docks. The result of one man's enthusiasm, this museum of advertising and packaging could be described as a century of shopping-basket history

63 The shop Beatrix Potter chose for her *Tailor of Gloucester* is now a museum too, with many exhibits of the author's life and work

64 The New Inn, in Northgate Street, Gloucester, was a fifteenth-century pilgrims' hostelry; it still has its courtyard and surrounding balconies

65 The Victorian schoolroom in the Gloucester Folk Museum, which is a museum of local history, folklore, crafts and industries housed in historic timber-framed Tudor buildings. The schoolroom holds 'period' lessons for those willing to learn!

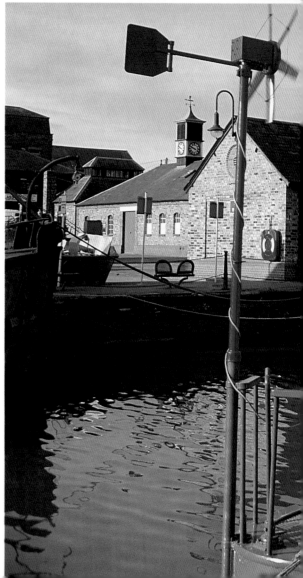

6 The National Waterways Museum at Gloucester Docks recreates
the remarkable story of Britain's inland waterways using working
engines, live craft demonstrations, workable models and
machinery, archive film, sound recordings and computer games

67 Prinknash Abbey (pronounced 'prinnage') was consecrated in 1972 and meets the needs of today's monks belonging to the ancient Benedictine order. Their pottery is famous, and the abbey grounds contain a bird park and medieval fish ponds

68 The old manor at Prinknash Abbey, St Peter's Grange, is a monastic retreat and continues to dispense Benedictine hospitality in accordance with the Benedictine rule

69 The flamingoes at the Wildfowl and Wetlands Trust, Slimbridge, are a colourful sight all year round. This is the world's largest collection of swans, geese, ducks and other water birds

70 Berkeley Castle is the perfectly preserved home of the family who built it 800 years ag

71 The Jenner Museum, in the grounds of Berkeley Castle, was the home of the famous physician who invented vaccination

THE ROYAL FOREST OF DEAN

Primeval forest once covered most of England so thickly that a squirrel with enough energy could have gone from the Severn to the Wash without setting foot upon the ground. The Royal Forest of Dean is a remnant of that ancient forest which, in 1016, was decreed in King Canute's Charta de Foresta to be a royal hunting ground. Even today 27,000 acres belong to the Crown and are available for visitors to enjoy.

Yet this 'Queen of Forests all', full of oaks, ash and other broadleaved forest trees of England, is also an industrial site. In the twelfth century, as the last approximation to the ancient wildwood in England, it was converted to coppiced woodland and wood-pasture, providing fuel for the local iron industry and grazing for livestock. The large quantities of timber at hand made the iron industry very successful in the Forest of Dean by the thirteenth century, when there were seventy-two furnaces in operation. St Briavels was a great armaments centre, but today it is probably better known for its Whit Sunday tradition of Bread and Cheese Dole.

Coal has been mined in the Forest of Dean for centuries (the names Coleford and Cinderford tell us that) and some of Britain's free mines are still worked here. The last of the stone-cutting factories and the last handmade brickworks continue to operate in the forest.

Clearwell Caves were worked for iron for more than 2,500 years until 1945. Today geological and mining displays reveal how the early miners worked and how techniques gradually evolved.

The iron industry declined in the forest when timber came to be used for shipbuilding and was no longer available to fuel the furnaces. But after 1795 coke was used to smelt the iron ore and Admiral Lord Nelson, in 1803, made 'strong and firm' recommendations for the planting of oaks there. They were duly planted and provided timber for the wooden minesweepers which cleared magnetic mines in the Second World War.

Dean Heritage Centre, near Cinderford, explains the story and heritage of the Royal Forest of Dean. There, in a former iron foundry, corn mill, leatherboard mill, timber yard, piggery and scrapyard, various exhibits describe the industries with the help of a reconstructed mine, a nineteenth-century coal miner's cottage, a Lightmoor Colliery Engine and a water wheel. The museum explores history and wildlife and the self-sufficient lifestyle of the forester, and there are three nature trails.

The Romans left their mark at Littledean Hall, where the remains of the Roman Springhead Temple reveal the largest restored ground plan of such a temple in Britain.

72 Springtime in the ancient Forest of Dean

73 Dean Heritage Centre has art and craft
exhibitions, nature trails, a shop and picnic sites

74 This cider mill is among the many interesting items showing the ways of yesteryear in the forest at Dean Heritage Centre. A beam engine and 3-metre (10 ft) overshot water-wheel can also be seen

75 The reconstructed forester's cottage at Dean Heritage Centre is just one of the things that tells the story of a forest and its people

76 The only railway station in the south of the Forest of Dean is at Lydney, where the Dean Forest Railway at the Norchard Steam Centre has full-sized railway engines and coaches and a museum display of drawings and photographs

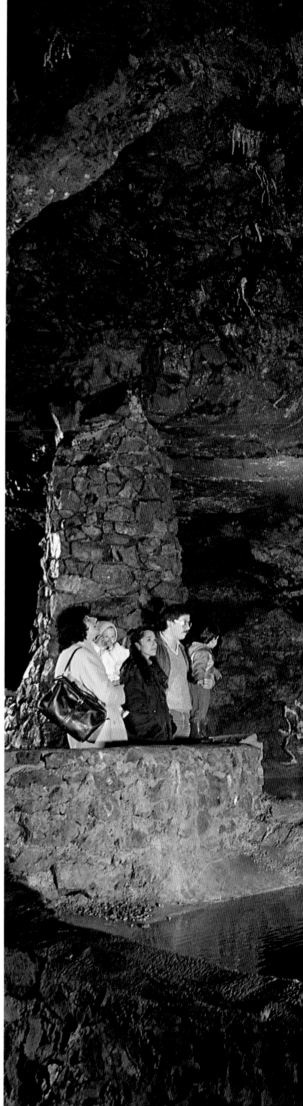

77 Iron ore has been mined in the forest for nearly 3,000 years and, at Clearwell Caves, there are eight large caverns open to the public. Displays and engines show the advances in mining techniques from the primitive to the modern

78 The preservation of a forest depends on good management and the Royal Forest of Dean is well cared for by the Forestry Commission which balances timber production with the need for nature conservation

79 Jubilee Maze was built in 1977 to celebrate the Silver Jubilee of Queen Elizabeth II. It is worth visiting the Museum of Mazes before attempting to find the way to the Temple of Diana at the centre of the maze

80 The view from Yat Rock over the Wye Valley and Royal Forest of Dean

81 Owned by the National Trust, Westbury Court Garden is a formal water garden laid out between 1696 and 1705. It is the earliest of its kind in England and was restored in 1971, only using varieties of plants available in 1700

32 The atmosphere of Victorian life is perfectly captured in
The Shambles of Newent, a collection of shops in cobbled streets,
alleys and squares, approached through a furnished four-storey
Victorian tradesman's house

33 The parterre at Westbury Court Garden has been replanted
using dwarf box, coloured sages and other plants that would have
been originally used in this early formal layout. It is one of the
finest examples in the country

84 Buckholt Wood National Nature Reserve is part of
Cranham Woods, a fine example of limestone
beechwoods lying near to Witcombe Roman Villa and to
the hill renowned for its annual 'cheese rolling'
competitions on Spring Bank Holiday Monday